Pearls and Pitfalls
of Medical Malpractice

Pearls and Pitfalls
of Medical Malpractice

Glen Joshpe, M.D.

To order, visit
www.avoidmalpractice.us

ISBN 978-1-4538-9578-8

10 9 8 7 6 5 4 3 2 1

ABOUT THE AUTHOR

Glen Joshpe, M.D., FAAFP, practiced Internal Medicine, Family Practice, and Geriatrics in Stamford, New York, in the Catskills for over 30 years. During this time, he served in many capacities, including member of the Health Systems Agency/Northeastern New York, President of the Delaware County Medical Society, and founding member of the Delaware County Hospital Association. He was Medical Director to the Community Hospital of Stamford, Robinson Terrace Skilled Nursing Facility, Otsego County ARC, and Stamford Family Practice of A.O. Fox Hospital. He has also served as a consultant and contributing writer for Hospital Underwriters Mutual (HUM), and developed its first Early Warning Alert System. His goal in writing this book is to illustrate some of the pearls and pitfalls to help avoid malpractice.

He retired in 2007, and lives with his wife Vicki in Florida.

To contact the author e-mail: gjoshpe@hotmail.com

ACKNOWLEDGMENT

Many thanks to Kent Joshpe for the cover and interior illustrations.

DISCLAIMER

Since this text is about liability prevention I would be remiss not to include the following disclaimer:

Although an effort has been made to describe realistic situations, under certain circumstances, the author reserves the right to invoke poetic license or modify actual events for the purpose of illustrating certain points. Therefore, no inference should be made attributing any comments or actions to any actual person, being living or dead.

Furthermore, the author is presenting his opinions from his years as a practicing physician, a past administrator and consultant in the field of medical liability. He is not an attorney nor is he offering legal advice. Readers should consult their own medical liability legal staff for such advice as well as the specific laws in the state where they practice.

To all those caring, competent, dedicated,
and hard-working physicians who have had the
misfortune to have their patients become the plaintiffs

Contents

Foreword

Many physicians believe that being sued is an inevitable part of practicing medicine, and if you haven't been sued, then you are either lucky or haven't been in practice long enough. Dr. Joshpe's accomplishment of practicing 35 years without a suit is an admirable feat. This primer illustrates that luck is not the key ingredient in avoiding malpractice. You will learn that there are key steps one can take to avoid malpractice suits and build trusting relationships with your patients.

I had the pleasure of growing up in Stamford, New York where Dr. Joshpe practiced for the majority of his career. During that time, he served as a role model, not only for me, but for many others. He has always been well liked and respected by his patients, and served in many volunteer organizations in our community.

Most physicians do not work in a small rural community whereby you are known and interact with most folks. However, regardless of where you practice, poor outcomes happen, and physicians, being human, will make mistakes. It is how you relate to your patients that most likely will determine if you will find yourself in court, as patients are much less likely to sue a physician that they respect and like.

Dr. Joshpe cites many examples of how a physician's documentation, or lack thereof, can have a significant effect on the outcome of events. The pearls and pitfalls discussed herein are pertinent, regardless of where you practice. In today's malpractice environment, if you are not taking these defensive measures you are risking a lawsuit. The first step in your defense is to read this book.

Matthew Stupple, M.D.
Former Medical Director of Emergency Services
Benedictine Hospital
Kingston, New York

Dr. Joshpe has written a well-organized text on best practices. It is far more inclusive than the title suggests. If one reads it carefully, the essence of the entire process of ideal medical care becomes patently obvious. The key to success is the ability to communicate. Every chapter in this highly organized series stresses both by direct pronouncement as well as by defined examples, the need to communicate: communicate with patients, with healthcare providers, with the legal system, and with health care resources, such as the insurance and pharmaceutical industries. He stresses the need to understand. Dr. Joshpe has made it unequivocally clear that attention to detail and the ability to communicate events and processes lead to efficient, worry-free care. He is to be commended for these efforts.

Samuel Gross, M.D.,
Professor Emeritus,
College of Medicine,
University of Florida

1

Introduction

IN 2007, AFTER 35 YEARS of practicing Internal Medicine and Family Practice, I decided to call it quits. I was indeed fortunate never to have a malpractice suit but I witnessed the devastating effects that they had on some of my colleagues. Most of them were excellent clinicians with good training, and yet that wasn't enough. In chapter six of this primer, one notes that a physician's malpractice experience has more to do with how one relates and communicates with patients, than with issues of training, education and experience.

My practice was in a small rural town, Stamford, New York, in the Catskill Mountains. Initially, I was Medical Director for the Community Hospital of Stamford, which was a full-service 29-bed acute care hospital, with a four-bed obstetrics unit, and a 40-bed skilled nursing facility. My outpatient practice was attached to the hospital.

Although I practiced my entire carreer in this village, I had the opportunity to wear many different hats, including solo practice and hospital-based group practice, and even a stint as CEO of our community hospital.

In 1975, Paul Decker, then Vice President of Hospital Under-writers Mutual (HUM)—since incorporated into MLMIC—and I worked to develop the first Risk Management program for their 171 hospitals. Since then, I have tried to make myself aware of the pearls and pitfalls that affect malpractice.

The practice of medicine has changed drastically since the previous generation of physicians. Three illustrations follow: In 1943, a woman entered Dr. Francis Brown's office in Hobart, New York, in Delaware County. The doctor recalled, "She wanted to sell me a malpractice insurance policy. I had never even heard that word previously, but I figured for $25 a year, how could I go wrong?"

In 1954, Ralph E. Betts, Administrator of Delaware Valley Hospital in Walton, NY, announced to the medical staff that they were now going to require a *separate chart* for each and every patient.

In 1971, I was reminiscing with an old-time GP in Monticello, New York. As a gentleman limped by, Dr. Burke said to me, "See that guy? I put a plate in his head." My first thought: Were they in a bar fight? "No, he had a tractor accident and was carried into the office. I had to excise a portion of his frontal lobe and put a plate in his head." This sounds more like the old Doc in *Gunsmoke* from Dodge City, rather than the 20th century. However, in rural areas in the '30s and '40s, that's the way it was. There were no interstate highways, medivacs to trauma centers, or even a credentialing process for delineated privileges, and there were no malpractice suits. The local Doc either patched you up or you died.

It's no longer your father's medical practice. Medicine has changed, and we need to change our thinking and methods as well. Actions and behaviors which may have been appropriate in the 1970s may not be relevant today. Patients and plaintiff attorneys are more sophisticated. They are able to research diseases, meds, side effects, etc. If outcomes aren't optimum, your patient may now become a plaintiff. We physicians are walking a very slippery slope. We need to learn how to protect ourselves, while still practicing quality care. During the past 35 years I have compiled these tips to help you negotiate these challenges.

PEARL AND PITFALL: Change with the times or your patient may become the plaintiff.

2

A Litigious Society

I RECENTLY HEARD ON TV, "If you have suffered an injury, as a result of a slip and fall, call the law firm of Morton and Morton." Wait a minute! He didn't say a "trip and fall," nor did he say "push and fall," not even a "shove and fall." Why is it that when someone slips on your property, it is your fault? Shouldn't an individual be responsible for knowing how to walk?

A neighbor's child tripped during play and injured an ankle. The family notified me that I should be expecting a summons. Kids play, they run, they fall, they sprain ankles, and occasionally break bones. Is this the fault of the ground or the property owner?

An uninsured drunk driver runs up on the sidewalk and injures a patient in an AT&T phone booth. A law suit is filed targeting AT&T's deep pockets. Was the phone booth at fault? A ball player sustains a head injury while wearing a protective helmet. Often, all one needs to demonstrate negligence is not to show that the helmet was constructed faultily, but that someone, somewhere, could have designed a helmet differently to possibly avert the injury. Manufacturers are reluctant to sell power tools or ladders due to the risk of injury, and when they are produced, the costs can be prohibitive. It has been said that if this pattern goes unchecked, a "white handkerchief" is all that will be "made in the USA."

Our society is out of control, and those in the medical profession are at the forefront of such unmerited and frivolous lawsuits. My carpenter cut a board two inches shorter than intended. He said, "Oops," and discarded the board and reached for another. I said to him, "You know John, that's the difference between carpentry and medicine. If you were a physician that would be a malpractice suit."

I recall a case whereby a nurse administering an allergy injection gave 0.1cc rather than .01cc. At first glance it may appear relatively innocuous, but in reality it is a tenfold error. However, let us imagine for a moment that it was your accountant who misplaced a single decimal point. After all, accountants handle hundreds of transactions daily, and we do not expect that they will never make an error. That is why they put erasers on pencils, isn't it? Would we haul such an accountant into court and subject him to defending his lifelong work? Would we subject him to public humiliation and the risk of financial ruin or license revocation?

Well guess what? Folks in the medical profession are also human, and yes, mistakes can and will occur. We physicians are required to make hundreds of decisions a day, including selecting drugs, calculating dosages, interpreting lab findings, recording data, etc. Often we are awakened from a sound sleep in the middle of the night and need to fire off a litany of drugs and dosages to treat life-threatening emergencies. And yet, we carry the burden of knowing that one error in judgment or omission may be a career-ending decision.

Our current tort system is out of control. It is punitive, unjust, and detrimental to society and the well-being of our patients. Drastic tort reform is imperative. A contingency system that allows attorneys to claim a third of the patient's settlement, including million-dollar awards for "pain and suffering," is ludicrous. The system should not provide an attorney with incentives to maximize the patient's "pain and suffering." Well-trained physicians who have dedicated their lives to helping others should not have to function under these conditions.

We shouldn't be surprised that many of the Congressmen writing these laws are attorneys who return to their firms after leaving Congress.

PEARL AND PITFALL: Take caution that a misplaced decimal point does not become the final blemish on an otherwise illustrious career.

The Doer vs. the Reviewers

Looking over the shoulder of today's physician: the JCAHO, HIPAA, OSHA, MC/MA, BC/BS, State Health Dept., the family and their attorney

3

Follow Your Policies, or Change Them

IF ONE WANTS TO FIND trouble quickly, simply have your office or hospital policy book at variance with what you actually do. For example, a patient in the nursing home on Coumadin developed a major bleed. Protimes were ordered monthly and within the desired range prior to the bleed. However, the nursing home policy book stated that Protimes should be ordered no less often than every two weeks. The policy had been in existence for years, even before the physician in question had joined the staff. Imagine the following courtroom scenario:

ATTORNEY: Doctor, do you have a methodology in your institution, which sets policies to be followed by the staff, to assure proper care?

MD: Yes.

ATTORNEY: And is that called the medical staff policy book?

MD: Yes.

ATTORNEY: And does that book delineate the proper and appropriate method for monitoring a patient's risk of bleeding when on Coumadin?

MD: Yes.

ATTORNEY: And would you kindly read to the jury the wording of that policy?

Get the point? Don't allow yourself to be placed in such a precarious situation.

First, whenever becoming involved in any institution, whether it is hospital- or office-based practice, read and familiarize yourself with the policy book. Many physicians are unaware that when they sign their application for privileges, there is a statement saying that they have read the rules and regulations and policies of the medical staff and the facility. As Medical Director and President of my medical staff for many years, I have always included the packet of policies to any member applying to our staff. Furthermore, at the time of recredentialing, staff members would again initial the policy book and any changes would be highlighted. In reality, I would suspect that many physicians are agreeing to follow policies and procedures that they have never even read.

Let's return to our example. Why have a policy regarding monitoring of Coumadin which is so restrictive? An alternative might be: "Patients on Coumadin should periodically have the dosage monitored for possible adjustment. (Guidelines from weekly to monthly, as clinically indicated.)" The previous doctor–attorney cross-examination would play out very differently under this scenario.

MD RESPONSE: Every patient is different, and no two doctors follow the exact same methodology for monitoring such cases. In my professional opinion, after monitoring this patient for years, I believe the course taken was correct and prudent.

We do need policies and they are required by a plethora of regulations, but let's not allow them to intimidate us into stating what we don't really do. Good medical care can't be found in a cookbook, but calls for guidelines, rather than absolute mandates.

Your hospital by-laws also need to follow the same advice. If your by-laws call for a physician's application to join your staff should be acted upon within 30 days of applying, don't allow six months to go by before taking action.

This advice pertains to your office as well. Review your policy book on a regular basis. Make sure it states what you actually do. Bring outdated policies, as well as those in need of change, to the appropriate committee for consideration of deletion or modification. Be sure to initial and date any changes in your policies.

PEARL AND PITFALL: Follow your policy book, or change your policy.

4

The ER: Never the Final Disposition

AS WE ARE ALL AWARE, treating patients in the Emergency Room carries an additional risk of liability, as well as other potential problems. Often, we are confronted with patients we have not previously treated, many of whom have no regular physician or preventive care, some of whom may be under the influence, and others who will never follow up once they leave the ER.

I was once involved in a case of a middle-aged woman who presented to the Emergency department with a knee injury. Physical exam and X-ray were unremarkable. I included in my written instructions to the patient, "RTO—1 week." (Abbreviation for, return to office, to be discussed in further detail in the chapter on abbreviation list). The next communication I had with her was through her attorney. He stated that I had failed to diagnose a tendon tear in her knee, and the patient was contemplating a malpractice suit. Further investigation revealed that the patient failed to keep her appointment for follow-up, and had actually sustained a separate injury weeks afterwards. After the attorney had reviewed my notes and learned the facts, the matter was dropped.

However, I cannot emphasize enough the importance of never having the ER be the final disposition of the patient. If one is acutely ill to the point of needing to go to the ER then they should require a follow-up visit to assure that the crisis has resolved. I have reviewed many ER records in which the physician could have avoided trouble by simply stating, "RTO—1 wk." If the patient's condition worsens after two weeks and they failed to follow up with you a week later as advised, whose liability is it? It may also be prudent to have the staff call the patient if they fail to show and document the response and time of the call. Furthermore, if family accompanies the patient, particularly for the elderly or impaired, have them witness the instructions.

Occasionally a note will say, "Follow up with your own MD." A more satisfactory approach would be, "Call your physician in the A.M. for a follow-up appointment." One cannot rely on the patient's judgment to know if a follow-up visit should be within a day, a week, or a year.

One also needs to explain to the patient the consequences of failing to follow your discharge instructions. In a landmark case, a patient's wife called the physician stating her husband was having chest pain. The physician told the wife to hang up and call 911, since the patient may be having a heart attack. The wife ignored the recommendation and the patient did indeed expire from a heart attack. The lawsuit against the physician blamed the physician for failing to say that a heart attack can be fatal.

Scheduling follow-up visits at an appropriate time not only applies to the ER. Surgeons should schedule a post-operative patient with a follow-up appointment within a week of surgery, when complications are most likely to occur, rather than a month later.

PEARL AND PITFALL: Never have the ER be the final disposition of the patient.

5

Your Best Care Is Your Routine Care

A FELLOW PHYSICIAN ONCE SAID TO ME, "Your best care is your routine care." And yet, we often believe that we can do even better when it comes to family and friends. As physicians we are all confronted with requests for medical advice during social gatherings. It reminds me of the story of a doctor and lawyer at a cocktail party, and everyone was asking the doctor questions but no one bothered the lawyer. The physician then asked the lawyer why no one questioned him. The lawyer responded, "When people ask me a question, I send them a bill for $100." The doctor said, "Great advice." The next day the physician received a bill from the lawyer for $100.

It's not as if we mind giving free advice. It's just that one cannot perform a proper evaluation in social settings. When a patient sticks a rash in your face during a cocktail party, you're not about to invoke the SOAP (subjective, objective, assessment and plan) methodology. Are you going to take a thorough history, including drug use, travel history, sun exposure, etc.? Are you going to whip out a flashlight to provide ideal visibility? Patients often believe that physicians are magicians, and can provide immediate resolution to problems. They are unaware that a somewhat scientific process is involved.

Often what patients are seeking under such circumstances is re-assurance. They want to hear a physician say, "It doesn't look like anything serious." On the other hand, what if it is? Are you going to put a bummer on the party by saying, "That looks like a malig-nant melanoma"? Giving casual advice or reassurance can turn out to be disastrous for the physician. The plaintiff's attorney will re-mind the jury that the patient received reassurance from a physi-cian and was not told that they had a potential life-threatening problem that was ignored.

Residing in a small town, I have been confronted with countless similar circumstances, whether at the supermarket or the gas sta-tion. I have adopted the following response: "I would like to discuss your concern in more detail. I have some questions but don't think we can go into it here and now. Why don't you either call my office tomorrow or make an appointment to see your own doctor?"

Giving advice to families can also backfire. We physicians need to be reminded that our loved ones are not immune from acquir-ing serious illnesses. A close relative phoned me and mentioned he had noticed blood in his stool. My first reaction in attempting to reassure him was to suggest that it was probably his hemorrhoid, as if casting doubts that a relative of mine cannot contract colon cancer. Would I react this way to any other patient? Of course not! They would have the benefit of my "routine care," including a rec-tal exam, colonoscopy, and GI workup. Try looking for short cuts and you may regret it.

PEARL AND PITFALL: Your best care is your routine care.

6

Bedside Manner vs. Do You Care?

WE ALL HEAR OUR PATIENTS DISCUSSING bedside manner, but what is it really? Is a good bedside manner giving the appearance of being a caring physician? Or is a good bedside manner actually caring? I believe that the patient can differentiate between the two. As a rural practioner, and one who treated 25 to 30 patients a day, I didn't spend a great deal of time on small talk. Sure, I would like to know the daily activities of my patients' kids, and how they were doing in Little League, soccer, etc. However, I don't believe that's why patients came to me. That also doesn't mean that I rushed patients or spent less time than necessary to investigate their complaints. They wanted the correct diagnosis, appropriate treatment and to be on their way ASAP. If a patient wanted to spend an excessive time schmoozing, I might say, "Why don't we get together after work, when we have more time?"

Please don't interpret this position as if I didn't care. Whenever a patient phoned me, I would always return their call quickly. When I would fall behind in my schedule, I would personally enter the waiting room and offer my apologies. As one who was rarely late, I have always considered the patients' time as valuable as my own. When the patient gave their history, I tried not to interrupt them.

My secretary Brenda would often send birthday and get-well greetings to many of our long-time patients. It was not in her job description and she wasn't reimbursed for it. She did it because she genuinely cared. When a patient of ours was seriously ill, we initiated a call the following day to check their progress and sent get-well cards to our hospitalized patients. If a patient passed away, we would attend the funeral.

I once had a dentist who always began our visit by asking the same two questions, "How's the family? How are the kids?" There was never any interaction or follow-up, as if the socialization part of our visit was now over. I wonder if he even heard my response.

I recall a patient named Ethel Fodder at Metropolitan Hospital in New York City, whom I treated during my Internship. The resident and I were completing a month rotation on the ward, and the patient became quite fond of us. The resident was an excellent physician with meticulous manners and always displaying the warmest greetings to the patient. When she learned that it was our last day, she asked if we would be back to visit her. The resident said, "Sure we will." I had stopped by several times subsequently, but my resident never did. Would you say he had a good bedside manner? Did he care?

The patient's belief that the physician doesn't genuinely care about their welfare contributes to the initiation of many malpractice suits. I recall one case where I was treating a patient, along with an oncologist, for metastatic carcinoma. During the patient's stay in the hospital under the care of the oncologist, I would call the family routinely to review the situation. For some reason, the oncologist and family were unable to develop a good rapport. The patient's condition deteriorated rapidly and the patient expired. The family became angry and approached me, stating they were considering suing the oncologist. After meeting with the family on several occasions, as well as attending the patient's funeral services, I was able to convince them that there was no basis for a suit.

In the nationally bestselling book, *Blink*, by Malcolm Gladwell, the author discusses (on pages 39 to 43) why some physicians are sued more than others. All physicians should read this chapter. The author points out that it is not the physician's training, expertise, or even how many mistakes the physician makes, but rather, how the physician personally interacts with his patient that is the most important factor in whether a physician is sued.

When the patient liked their physician they rarely initiated a suit. The physicians who cared, showed empathy, returned calls, listened well, and did not *talk down* to patients were not the ones who were generally sued. The author refers to a study conducted by Wendy Levinson who recorded hundreds of conversations between physicians and patients. Approximately half had never been sued and the other half had been sued at least twice. Those never sued spent at least three minutes longer with their patients than the other group. Another study examined only the doctor's tone of voice, and was able to successfully predict which physicians were to be sued.

PEARL AND PITFALL: The key isn't just bedside manner, it's caring. In spite of a busy schedule, we must convey to the patient that we are genuinely interested in their welfare.

7

You Never Know When

WE ALL HAVE THOSE PATIENTS with whom we feel totally relaxed, with whom we have an excellent rapport, and could never imagine them as a plaintiff. However, you never know. I can recall one case in which I treated a patient in an adult home for over 20 years. He was an elderly retired farm hand and very pleasant and appreciative of my care. One could bet the farm that the care of this patient would never terminate in a lawsuit.

One day he came into the ER in cardiogenic shock, experiencing a massive myocardial infarction. While I was tending to him, the nurse stated that his wife was in the waiting room and demanding to speak with me. "Wife, what wife? Johnnie isn't married." It turned out that Johnnie had been separated from his wife for over 20 years and she was uninvolved in his daily affairs. Now, in the ER, she suddenly appeared making demands.

I informed her that his condition was very critical and his prognosis guarded. The options were to treat him in a small community hospital in our two bed CICU, or transfer him to a medical center 60 miles away. She opted for the transfer. As the patient entered the ambulance, her parting words were, "If he dies en route, I'll see you in court."

PEARL AND PITFALL: Regardless of your rapport with the patient, never believe that you are immune from a suit. Your loyal and devoted patient may not be around to testify on your behalf.

8

Keep It in QA

WHEN CONGRESS ENACTED the Medicare program in 1965, it became apparent that a mechanism was needed to develop and evaluate quality medical standards. The initial goal was to assure that reimbursed services were medically necessary and performed as economically as possible.

In 1971, Congress authorized the Experimental Medical Care Organizations (EMCOs), again to control costs. Public Law 98–369 provided hospitals the right to develop Quality Assurance Committees whereby matters of quality of medical care could be evaluated in a confidential matter without fear of recrimination or retrievability in the courts under subpoena. After all, if such discussions were not protected, individuals would be reluctant to discuss sensitive matters openly.

You may ask, what does this have to do with me and the issue of malpractice? The answer is, plenty. Many physicians, as well as hospital officials, are unaware that what is discussed in the QA Committee is *privileged information*. Therefore, it is imperative when discussing problems and concerns of quality care that such meetings be held under the umbrella of your QA Committee, as opposed to an *open* meeting of your medical staff. Subsequent to the QA Committee meeting, the medical staff, in an *open* meeting, may make recommendations on specific matters, such as, "The QA committee recommends that Dr. J.'s surgical privileges be restricted and he is required to consult with another staff surgeon, prior to performing appendectomies."

Whenever conducting such meetings, I specifically point out to the recording secretary that the minutes should reflect that we are meeting as the Quality Assurance Committee. Although a plaintiff's attorney cannot subpoena the QA minutes, you could be asked as to what *you* specifically said during the meeting. If asked such a question, hopefully you will be able to respond with, "Yes, yes, no, no, yes!"

Incident reports, however, may be subject to subpoena, and they should not be discussed in the general medical record.

PEARL AND PITFALL: Keep your negative comments where they belong: in the QA Committee.

9

Completing the Circle: What Credentialing Is All About

AS A CONSULTANT TO HUM in the 1970s I found that many physicians really did not comprehend the methodology and goals of the credentialing process. I became enlightened about the process during a State Health Department survey. When the inspector had noticed that a skin biopsy from a surgeon had persistent tumor at the resected edges he asked me, as President of the Medical staff, what had been done about it. I was perplexed. "What do you mean?" I asked. He replied, "Where did this information go? What action was taken as a result?" These were all legitimate questions, to which I had an inadequate response. In reality, my action was similar to that taken by many hospital committee audits, which is often, *finish, file, and forget*. What the inspector wanted was proof that the circle had been completed.

Allow me to describe how the system should properly function. Throughout the year, the medical staff has a vast variety of committee meetings, i.e., infection control, antibiotic usage, surgical tissue review, pharmacy usage, QA, audit, etc. The purpose of such meetings is to review care and identify potential problems or discrepancies from desired outcomes. When such problems are identified action needs to be taken. How should this be done?

Each and every member of your staff needs to have a confidential credentials file. This file needs to be kept under lock and key in the administrator's office. All of these deviations from expected outcomes need to be forwarded to this confidential folder by the chairman of the various committees.

When the credentialing committee meets for the annual re-credentialing meeting, the committee reviews each individual file for compliance. In addition to proof of licensing, evidence of malpractice insurance, proof of CME, documentation of current health status, etc., the committee should review quality-care issues from all of the data on each physician, and then the committee should make recommendations to the medical staff and eventually to the Board of Directors regarding re-credentialing. The committee should identify *patterns of care*. If a physician performs ten appendectomies and has one normal appendix, that is very different from the one who has five undesirable results. In the latter case, an apropriate recommendation might be for that physician to obtain a pre-operative consult from another staff surgeon. Perform such actions, along with follow-up studies, and now the circle has been completed.

The appropriate response to the surveyor's inquiry in this example should have been, "This information, as well as over-all patterns of care, has been forwarded to our Credentialing Committee for review and/or action."

If you and your institution are not following this process, then you are missing the purpose of the credentialing process, as well as increasing your risk for litigation in the future.

PEARL AND PITFALL: When quality issues are identified, be sure to close the loop.

10

Granting Privileges: Who Verifies?

A SURGEON PRACTICED in one of two local hospitals. When he applied for similar credentials in the other, they were granted expeditiously. The Credentials Committee assumed that the surgeon was adequately credentialed in the previous institution, and didn't see the need to repeat the entire process in detail again.

When the surgeon's care proved to be substandard, subsequent investigations revealed there were warning signs in the past. Not only was the physician subsequently named in a malpractice suit, but the new hospital was as well.

The question was asked in court, what *independent verification* was done to check the physician's references and training? The Chairman of the Credentialing Committee took the position that the previous hospital had already checked the surgeon's credentials. The court ruled against the hospital, stating that it is each hospital's responsibility to perform an independent review.

Ever since learning of this case, I have always made it a practice to speak with references personally rather than rely on others.

PEARL AND PITFALL: When granting privileges, perform your own *independent verification* of references.

11

Screening Guidelines: Help or Hindrance

THESE DAYS EVERY SPECIALTY PROVIDES screening guideline time schedules for various procedures (i.e. mammography, paps, colonoscopy, etc.) Not only do many of these recommendations conflict with one another but they can also introduce one more source of litigation. The American Society of Gastroenterology recommends that all patients have a screening colonoscopy at age 50. In reality the percentage of Americans who strictly adhere to such guidelines are in the minority. Should the responsibility to comply with these recommendations fall totally with the physician? According to some plaintiff's attorneys, their answer is, "yes."

Let us examine the following case. A family physician departed from a group practice and was replaced by another colleague. The new physician had taken over the patient's care when she was 53 years old. The previous physician had seen the patient on occasion for problems unrelated to the GI tract. There was no documentation in the record of a colonoscopy being discussed when the patient turned 50.

Several months after the new physician entered the picture the patient developed GI symptoms. A work-up revealed advanced colon cancer from which the patient subsequently expired. The family sued, not the original physician since the statute of limitations had expired, but the new physician who diagnosed the problem. The case was settled out of court.

Now if this is considered to be malpractice, which I do not believe it is, who amongst us is not guilty? Are we physicians legally responsible to see that each and every patient who ever enters our office is in strict compliance with such arbitrary and capricious guidelines which even the specialists cannot agree upon? Are we also responsible for the patient who occasionally presents with an acute care problem, and yet does not care to have routine or preventive care? At what point does the patient assume responsibility for his or her own welfare?

In spite of the absurdity of this case, allow me to suggest some strategies for possibly averting such a disaster. Prepare a newsletter for your patients. Review all of these guidelines therein. State in your newsletter that the patient should inform your staff when they are due for each procedure so that they may be scheduled for you. Furthermore, have a bulletin board in your waiting room where all of this information is available.

The policy which was actually followed in the previously discussed case made matters even worse. The Medical Director of this 20-physician group that practiced at several different locations stapled the checklist form on the inner cover of every patient's chart. The form listed all of those screening procedures previously mentioned along with tetanus, and immunization timelines, which the physicians were asked to complete. The majority of the medical staff viewed this form as just one more unnecessary form to address, since each had devised their own system for monitoring these issues. Since the form was physically attached to the patient's chart, it then became a portion of the legal medical record, and ignoring the form gave the false impression that none of the recommendations were followed. A better alternative would have been to give each physician a single copy of the guidelines, which was available for their review, rather than physically attach it to the medical record.

When the case went to litigation, the plaintiff's attorney asked that the physician read aloud every one of the dozen items listed and then read his notation next to each. The form was blank. Just imagine how a jury would interpret this!

PEARL AND PITFALL: Communicate screening guidelines to your patients via a newsletter and waiting room bulletin board. Don't place unnecessary forms in the medical record that are not completed.

12

Utilize an Abbreviation List

I HAVE ALWAYS UTILIZED an official abbreviation list within my office policies. Not only has this practice saved much valuable time, I believe it can also decrease your liability risk. Obviously it is important to use a specific abbreviation for only one meaning, that is, when using OD, are you referring to once a day, or the right eye?

Let me discuss one specific example. In my abbreviation book is listed "RABs," which I define as Risks, Alternatives, and Benefits, including the risk and benefit of no treatment at all.

We are all reminded that when recommending or commencing a new treatment, or starting a new drug, the physician needs to review the risks, alternative treatments, and potential benefits with the patient. We also know that although we have such discussions with the patient on a regular basis, it is difficult, as well as time-consuming, to document each of these discussions into the medical record.

For example, assume that you have recommended that a patient begin Lipitor for hypercholesterolemia. You would then have a discussion about the potential side effects, discuss alternative medications, changes in lifestyle, weight reduction, and avoidance of smoking, and you also mention that drug therapy isn't for everyone, and that some patients can have side effects, such as liver dysfunction and muscle pain, including a more serious form called rhabdomylosis, whereby muscle breakdown can damage the kidneys. You mention that failure to treat may result in risk of early heart disease, stroke, or possible premature death.

Now assume that you have discussed all of this and more with your patient. Now you also have to document the discussion because you recall the adage, "If you don't document it, you didn't do it. " Imagine documenting, verbatim, every single discussion regarding the care of every patient throughout the day. Perhaps physicians will need a legal stenographer to accompany them into the exam room In the future. My alternative is to state in my notes, "Lipitor started, RABs discussed, including muscle and liver damage." Is this a foolproof technique? Possibly not. However, it does demonstrate my awareness and need to discuss treatment options and side effects with patients.

PEARL AND PITFULL: Develop your own abbreviation list. It will save time and may reduce liability.

13

Where Did "Rule Out" Go?

THIRD-PARTY REIMBURSEMENTS have had an enormous impact on our approach to the practice of medicine. As a resident physician in the '70s, I typically made notes such as this one:

Impression: R/O Pneumonia
R/O TBC
R/O PE
R/O CA lung

Notice that I used the word *impression* rather than *diagnosis*.

The prior tendency was to list your impressions in order of the most likely to the less likely. The list most likely contained the correct specific diagnosis, which would be obtained after the appropriate workup. Nowadays, with third-party regulators, such as Medicare, carriers will not reimburse providers without a specific diagnosis. If one orders a TSH and uses R/O hypothyroidism, Medicare will not approve the requisition. The potential consequences of this subtle change may provide the plaintiff's attorney with just another weapon.

Imagine the plaintiff's attorney saying, "Doctor, your diagnosis stated that the patient had pneumonia. However, the autopsy report indicates a pulmonary embolus." We physicians are being pressured and manipulated into stating a definitive diagnosis, prior to having an opportunity to complete the workup. To avoid such a trap, allow me to suggest an alternative approach. I would recommend making the following notation:

> Impression: pneumonia. Also need to consider and rule out TBC, PE, and CA, if symptoms and findings do not resolve.

In this manner you have demonstrated that all of the listed diseases are being considered in your approach to the patient.

PEARL AND PITFALL: Our ability to practice sound medicine is being adversely affected by the plethora of excessive regulation and management of our care. Don't allow regulators to pressure you into stating a specific diagnosis prematurely; include *rule out* in your notes.

14

Early Warning Alert Signs: Think *Defense*, and Document

EACH OF US MAY HAVE our own concept as to what constitutes *defensive medicine*. Although I personally advocate practicing *defensive medicine*, that doesn't mean I encourage ordering unnecessary and superfluous tests and procedures. Every child who bumps his head is not in need of a CT scan.

In the game of football, it has been said that the best defense is a good offense. The analogy holds true for the practice of medicine as well. A physician needs confidence and skills to make appropriate decisions, and without this, no defense will be adequate.

My conception of good *defensive medicine* is to act in the best interest of the patient while providing the documentation to support your reasoning and actions. If for any reason, results are less than desired, a rational person (or jury), will be able to follow and support your decision-making process.

The statements and actions by some patients raise our antennae that impending troubles may lay ahead, and when we have these feelings it is especially crucial to think defensively. For example, you inform the patient that since he has now reached the age of 50, you recommend he have a screening colonoscopy. The patient responds with, "I don't know, let me think about it, and get back to you." Do you respond by saying, "OK," and take no further action? Some physicians may do just that. My response would be, "These guidelines were adopted to detect polyps or colon cancer in early stages when they are readily treatable. So if you don't want to schedule the test at this time, I would ask that you initial my note in your chart stating your decision."

Perhaps you have a poorly compliant patient who misses appointments often or fails to take his or her medications as prescribed, or doesn't follow other suggested recommendations. If you are going to continue caring for such a patient, I would recommend that you specifically document this lack of compliance in your medical record. When confronted with the habitually noncompliant patient, one should also consider taking the appropriate measures to discharge the patient from your practice.

If the patient subsequently develops colon cancer, neither the patient nor the family will be able to state that you never informed them of the need for the procedure. This is what I am referring to when I recommend *defense.*

PEARL AND PITFALL: When your patient's actions raise a red flag, it is especially crucial to think *defensively.*

15

When Your Records Are Subpoenaed

WHEN YOUR RECORDS ARE SUBPOENAED or requested by any third party, one should be knowledgeable about what should, as well as what should not be sent. Your personal notes and observations should NOT be sent. If included in the general record, you may use a marker to black out the copy that includes this information. Then write and initial, next to the blackout, that these are your personal notes and observations.

A more preferential approach would be to keep such comments separate from your general notes. One recommendation is as follows: When dictating, state to the recorder that the following comments should be typed only on a form which has a heading in bold capital letters, **PERSONAL NOTES AND CONFIDENTIAL OBSERVATIONS—DO NOT COPY—DO NOT RELEASE**. I would recommend a different color paper for such notes making it more difficult for your staff to inadvertently copy such records.

Some comments that fall into this category are:

- Mom has no control of her kids; they are running around the waiting room and jumping on the furniture

- Staff notes a smell of alcohol on the patient's breath during his 10 A.M. visit
- As I entered the exam room, the patient was opening my cabinet drawers
- The patient is poorly groomed and has an obnoxious body odor

Releasing such comments to the patient will have an adverse effect on your relationship with them and if this patient were considering becoming a plaintiff at some future point, such comments may influence that decision.

Another portion of your records that should not be released are those records sent to you by the patient's previous physician. One needs to send only the records since you have initiated care.

Furthermore, any reference to HIV, or drug or alcohol addiction, should be excluded from your general notes. Release of such information requires that the patient sign a specific release requesting this information. Failure to comply, and releasing such information unknowingly, may become a source of litigation.

Whenever your records are sent to any third party, a copy of the requisition should be saved along with documentation as to where and when they were sent, and by whom.

Finally, anytime your records are subpoenaed and you suspect potential litigation, you need to notify your insurance carrier IMMEDIATELY.

PEARL AND PITFALL: Keep your personal notes and comments separate from your general records.

16

Alter the Medical Record
and You Will Stand Alone

IF YOU TAKE JUST ONE PEARL from this text, let it be: NEVER, NEVER, NEVER alter the medical record. Not only is it immoral but it is illegal and may result in criminal charges. When confronted with criminal charges, you are no longer being represented by your insurance carrier. It will become necessary for you to hire your own criminal attorney at your expense. If one is found guilty of felonious fraud you risk censorship and revocation of your medical license, fines, and even possible incarceration.

Furthermore, if this is a case going to litigation, you can rest assured that you will be caught. Sophisticated scientific techniques can distinguish ink dating, paper pressures, and various types of ink color and texture. If your records are electronically recorded, the computer will record the exact date and time your entries were made.

In one particular case, the physician failed to make any entries in the record regarding completing a diagram showing the abnormal findings on a form of the female anatomy. After being confronted by a potential suit, the physician then added entries to the form after the fact. However, he was unaware of the fact that the patient had already requested and received a copy of the form without such entries. Under such circumstances, all hope for the physician's defense dissipated.

If you discover an error of omission or an incorrectly typed statement, the correct procedure is to draw a single line through the error, write correction of error, along with the time and date of your entry, and then insert the correction. For example: The patient is taking Lopressor 25mg daily. (Error—should read Lotensin, corrected, 3/15/09, 1:15 A.M. (Place a single line through Lopressor.)

PEARL AND PITFALL: NEVER, NEVER, NEVER ALTER THE MEDICAL RECORD, or you may be standing naked (without the support of your insurance carrier).

17

Employing a Mid-level May Double Your Liability

DURING MY YEARS OF PRACTICE, I had the opportunity to work with over a dozen mid-level providers, both physician assistants and nurse practioners. Although the vast majority of them have been well trained and are competent, they do introduce a significant risk of liability to the supervising physician.

In the case of PAs especially, since nurse practioners have somewhat more independence, this liability is enhanced by the tendency of many hospitals to locate PAs in remote rural areas with minimal to negligible supervision. PAs are not independent practitioners and most function under the direct supervision of a licensed physician.

Although it has been deemed that the supervising physician does not necessarily need to be physically present in the building, locating mid-levels in remote areas without supervision for the purpose of extending the institution's market share or enhancing revenue, in my opinion, is unwise. Many such *supervisors* are supervisors in name only and are not reviewing and discussing cases as intended.

During a routine Medicaid audit, the inspector disallowed all of the reimbursements billed through my PA, stating that I had not provided proof of proper supervision. When I produced a separate journal listing the names and diagnoses of each patient seen, followed by my signature and date on a daily basis stating *reviewed and discussed*, all of his concerns were satisfied. This approach not only resolved the financial issues, but it also reduced liability.

Any physician working with a PA needs to be aware that the PA can only provide those services that are consistent with their training and credentialing, and furthermore, such procedures must also be consistent with the supervising physician's privileges and training. I recall one instance when a PA with some surgical experience was revising the distal tuft of a partially-amputated digit. The supervising physician was an internist without surgical privileges; surely, a disaster waiting to happen.

Lack of adequate supervision is not the only liability risk of working with mid-level providers. If a PA is your employee, the risk is magnified, since one is generally responsible for any employee's actions, regardless if they are or are not in the medical industry, under the doctrine of *respondent superior*. (Latin for "let the master answer.") This doctrine states that the employer is responsible for the actions of one's employees. Even if the PA is not your direct employee, but employed directly by an institution, with you as the supervisor, you still could be liable for their actions.

As a hospital-based physician in a satellite clinic, the hospital Administrator urged me to supervise a PA at the clinic. He preferred a PA for cost containment, as opposed to hiring another physician. Consenting to such a request would have compromised my time with my own patients and increased my liability. Furthermore, he offered me no additional consideration or compensation. I refused the offer.

When the concept of mid-level providers was initiated, it was the intent to assist physicians in managing some of their routine, uncomplicated matters. This would free up the physicians time to deal with more complex matters. In theory, this sounds fine. However, in medicine one never knows in advance when the patient's apparently innocuous symptoms become a serious and complex case. Allow me to illustrate:

- A sore throat in a child turns out to be a post pharyngeal abscess
- A routine headache is temporal arthritis and the patient goes on to blindness
- A mole turns out to be a malignant melanoma
- A patient recently developing insomnia and a sense of gloom suddenly commits suicide
- A routine "belly ache" turns into an acute surgical abdomen
- A patient with an eye infection has a herpes infection which causes blindness
- A child with discomfort in the leg has undiagnosed Ewing sarcoma of the femur

Do you get my point? In the practice of medicine one can never predetermine the simple from the complex cases. I am in no way advocating that we physicians should not work with mid-level providers. I simply want to raise the point that when you do, their errors are your errors. Their liability is also your liability, and it is not only their license that is in jeopardy, but yours as well. Finally, do not lose sight of the fact that when you agree to supervise a mid-level, you must notify your state health department as well as your insurance carrier.

PEARL AND PITFALL: When supervising mid-level practioners, the quality of their work reflects the quality of your work, and their liability is yours as well.

18

The True Cost of Malpractice

IF YOU HAVE READ WHAT HAS PRECEDED, and you are asking, "Why should I worry about this since I carry malpractice insurance?" then you do not comprehend the degree of anguish and pain that one experiences when involved in a malpractice suit. The initiation of such a suit can be a life-altering experience, and certainly not for the better. It is difficult to comprehend all of the ramifications that may follow.

Loss of reputation, as well as self-confidence, loss of time and income from EBTs (Examination Before Trial) and court appearances, as well as a decrease in patients from adverse publicity, are some of the overlooked effects of a malpractice suit. In addition, a suit may cause untold mental stress, leading to self-doubt, depression, insomnia, or other health-related problems.

As physicians, we make hundreds of decisions on a daily basis and effective functioning requires a degree of confidence in one's abilities. If lost, the results may be paralyzing and result in an inability to make clinical decisions. A physician cannot request a consultation or referral on every case.

Some examples of a loss of confidence follow. I received a call at home from the ER nurse, stating that "Something is wrong! The attending physician is spending 45 minutes treating a URI." In another instance, a well-trained family doc suddenly began to document notes excessively, paced himself considerably slower, and demonstrated a loss of pleasure in his work.

How many other physicians have either left practicing medicine to turn towards teaching or administrative roles as a result of a malpractice suit? How many physicians have given up surgery or obstetrics either because of litigation or unwillingness to pay six figures in premiums for the privilege of performing these services?

The financial strains of a malpractice suit can be devastating. Although most cases are settled within the limits of the physician's coverage, there is no certainty of that. Furthermore, one could have all their assets legally tied up by a lien pending the results of a suit. This could delay or affect the physician's plans for retirement, as one's ability to retrieve assets are impeded.

If, after reading what has preceded, your response is that I'm not about to alter things that I have done for years, well then I seriously advise you to reconsider. Perhaps you have been fortunate to date, but don't become a disaster waiting to happen.

PEARL AND PITFALL: A little extra bit of time can be an ounce of protection as opposed to a pound of cure. Don't underestimate the full cost and stress of a malpractice suit.

19

The High-Risk Patient

ONE EFFECTIVE TOOL IN AVOIDING malpractice is to identify the *high-risk* patient before the fact; not *high risk* for disease, but *high risk* for litigation. When presented with a potential new patient, prior to entering the exam room, I would have a discussion with him or her in the conference room. During the meeting I would inform the patient that this is an opportunity to get to know each other and to see if we are compatible and willing to enter a *doctor-patient relationship*.

This relationship is a unique one and carries specific legal rights and responsibilities. Once the physician enters this agreement, certain steps need to be followed prior to discharging the patient. To do so, one needs to provide them with a minimal 30-day notice (preferably by certified mail), be available to treat them during that period, and provide them with a list of alternative physicians. Failure to do so runs the risk for a charge of patient abandonment. Discharging a patient that you have previously accepted can also become source of stress and additional aggravation.

Be informed, however, that you are not required to enter into a *doctor-patient relationship* if you are not comfortable for any reason. If you find yourself getting "bad vibes" from the patient, do not be reluctant to pass. Here are some examples which may raise your antennae:

- The *doctor-hopping* patient, who has had a half-dozen physicians in the past few years because none of them knew what they were doing.
- The *non-complier*, with a history of not following her doctor's advice, and not keeping appointments.
- *The lister*, who has amassed a long list of diseases that he believes he has, along with a theory on how they should be managed.
- The *attention seeker*, who requires lots of time to listen to all of the details of his or her life and family. One such elderly patient I had came to me after *bad-mouthing* her previous physician. With each visit she would describe all of the details of her grandchildren's lives, and show photos. I would patiently listen, and she told everyone she met what a great doctor I was. One day I was behind schedule, and had to cut her short. She stormed out, changed doctors, and bad-mouthed me to everyone. Why didn't I recognize the signs?
- The *flirtatious* patient. Watch out! If you have such a patient, you had better have your nurse accompany you into the exam room on every visit.
- The *multiple accidents injured* patient. After years of practice I try to avoid this patient. They often have more than one suit against multiple carriers, including workmen's compensation. Often they present with a plethora of forms for you to complete, along with a request for narcotics, and there is a possibility that you could be asked to testify on injuries sustained prior to your

involvement. I had one such patient with three separate prior work-related back accidents. Six different attorneys were involved at the hearing. I was asked, under oath, to testify regarding the percentage of disability from each case. I didn't try to impress anyone with my knowledge, and open myself to a cross-examination which I couldn't defend. My response: "There is no way for me to determine that and I have no idea."

If and when you tell such a patient that you don't believe you are the best physician for him, he may respond by asking, "Can you just refill my Vicodin, until I can obtain an appointment with another physician?" Do not fall into this trap. Once you have written a prescription for that patient, a *doctor-patient relationship* has been established.

• The *hypochondriac* patient may present with a list of symptoms that include at least one item from each category in the review of systems. When such a patient presents with real pathology a physician's dismissive attitude may allow it to go undetected. Also, never state in your notes that the patient is a hypochondriac. If you miss something, their attorney will highlight the fact that you didn't take their symptoms seriously. When confronted with such a patient, my notes may state, "On some other occasions the patient has presented with symptoms for which a thorough workup failed to find any demonstrable organic pathology."

PEARL AND PITFALL: If your vibes tell you that you are confronting a high-risk patient, think twice before entering into a *doctor-patient relationship.*

20

Who Is Following Up?

MANY MALPRACTICE SUITS ORIGINATE due to a failure to follow up on abnormal findings. When several providers are involved in the care of the patient, who bears the responsibility to assure proper followup?

All physicians should be aware of the differentiation between a consult and a referral. With a consult, the primary physician is requesting an evaluation and an opinion. The definitive responsibility of followup rests with the primary. In the case of a referral, the primary is sending the patient to another physician or specialist to take over the role of diagnosis, treatment, and followup in that specific arena. For example: as an Internist, Family physician, and Geriatrician, I referred all of my GYN care to a gynecologist. The responsibility for treatment and followup would rest with the the GYN.

Unfortunately, many patients have become lost in the shuffle. An abnormal pap is reported, and each physician assumes the other will follow up. When dealing with hospitalized patients, I would suggest that when ordering a consult from a specialist, your order should be specific, and say, infectious disease consult only, or Infectious disease consult and treat.

It becomes imperative that every physician develop a system for followup on labs, X-rays, and reports. The physician should date, insert any comments, and initial. Some physicians are now relying on e-mail to notify patients. I can foresee some potential danger with this process. Did the patient receive the information in a timely fashion? Can confidentiality be assured? Does the patient have an opportunity to ask questions and discuss options?

PEARL AND PITFALL: Many malpractice suits are caused by failure to follow up. Review your office policies to assure that your system is airtight.

21

Focus on What You Do Well

A NEIGHBOR REFERRED A PATIENT with a rash to me. After my exam, I informed the patient that I did not know the diagnosis or treatment, and referred him to a dermatologist 60 miles away. When I next saw my neighbor, he stated that his friend was very impressed with me. "You're kidding," I said, "I told him that I had no idea what was wrong with him." He responded, "That is why he was impressed."

Furthermore, whenever the patient or family either states or implies that they would be more comfortable with a second opinion, insist that a consult be obtained. One of the reasons that some physicians find themselves in hot water is because they try to extend their area of expertise. I knew of one such family doc, who was quite knowledgeable, and treated 25 to 30 patients a day. He performed some surgical procedure, such as herniorrhaphies, practiced OB, and cared for newborns. He also managed most of his complicated medical cases, rarely requesting consultation. In my opinion, such a physician would have provided a greater service by requesting a consult from an Internist, when managing acutely ill complex medical cases.

If you are one of those physicians who attempt to push the envelope to the max: Beware! When faced with a patient whose needs are beyond your routine skills, either request a consult or refer the patient.

PEARL AND PITFALL: Focus on what you do well.

22

Bad-Mouth a Colleague, and You
May Just Put Your Foot in It

A PATIENT WAS HOSPITALIZED with a ruptured appendix. A passing physician said, "Why don't you sue? That is why physicians carry malpractice insurance." The flippant comment not only got back to the primary physician, but the malpractice carrier as well, which insured both physicians. The physician who made the comment no longer practices in the state.

In another incident, a physician speaking at an open county medical society meeting urged colleagues to boycott another physician specialist, accusing him of incompetence. Make such accusations and you may find yourself in court defending charges of defamation of character.

Never bad-mouth or blame another healthcare professional for a complication, whether it is another physician, a nurse, or any staff member. Never attribute a bad result to the hospital or its cost containment program.

Occasionally, a physician will acquire a new patient who has the need to bad-mouth the previous physician. If you try to make points with the patient by agreeing with them, you may regret it, as you could one day be called upon to defend your remarks. Don't allow yourself to fall into this trap. If the patient has negative comments regarding your predecessor, simply state, "Well, I wasn't around to witness what happened in the past, so let's just start from scratch, and see if I can be of help."

PEARL AND PITFALL: Bad-mouth a colleague and you may just put your foot in it.

23

Out of the Office Doesn't Mean Out of Risk

THE PRACTICE OF MEDICINE OFFERS unique challenges in many ways. In what other field does one find themselves at risk, 24/7? Even when sleeping, one never knows when an emergency call from a nurse will suddenly require one to awaken and fire off a litany of life-saving orders. In most fields of work, one has the luxury to relax the mind at day's end. Not only is this not the case for physicians, but the liability risks also never ends.

The problem is magnified by the fact that the physician's best defense against malpractice is often proof of adequate documentation. Yet, how does one document responding to a patient's phone call when out of the office or during a social engagement, or when responding to a patient's question at the supermarket or gas station?

I have found that the carbon copy note pads distributed by my insurance carrier have been extremely helpful in this regard. I keep one on my office desk, one in my car, and a third on my night stand. Whenever responding to a patient interaction, I document the discussion, and my advice on these pads, noting the time and date, and then initialing. When taking calls for other colleagues, a copy of the note is forwarded to them as well. A copy of each note is placed in the patient's chart and when the pads are completed, they are filed by date.

PEARL AND PITFALL: We physicians would never consider treating patients in our office without any documentation. Therefore why consider it out of the office, where liability is just as real?

24

Nursing Home Pitfalls: Pain Control, Psychotropics, Restraints, and Falls

IN THE PAST, A NURSING HOME practice was an area of relatively low liability. Today that is no longer true. Adequate pain control, use of psychotropics, restraints, and patient falls contribute to looming pitfalls for physicians caring for patients in nursing homes.

As health care providers, we have all been inundated with the requirement to measure the fifth vital sign, quantifying the level of pain. As with the implementation of many new policies, legal issues have initiated the change. In a landmark case, a family sued a nursing home physician for failure to provide adequate pain relief to a patient with end-stage pancreatic carcinoma. The plaintiffs won the case.

Once again, the physician is being tugged in opposite directions simultaneously. Paradoxically, we have been criticized for prescribing excessive narcotics in the past and now we are being held liable for inadequate pain control.

Furthermore, nursing home (as well as hospital) providers need to be aware of the latest Federal and State regulations and standards of care when prescribing major psychotropic agents. They

include: schizophrenia, schizo-affective disorder, delusional de-
mentia, psychotic mode disorder, acute psychotic episode, Tourette's
disorder, Huntington's chorea, and organic mental disorders, such
as delirium.

When prescribing medications for these disorders one needs to
indicate the specific behavior being targeted. Omitting this makes
it difficult or impossible to know if the medication is effective or
not. This becomes even more important when a new physician
takes over care. The new physician may be reluctant to alter the
medication if unaware why it was prescribed. For example, if the
drug was prescribed because the patient was "biting staff'" and the
patient no longer displays this behavior, then the new physician
should consider modifying the medication.

When prescribing these medications, one needs to attempt to
use the lowest effective dosage, implement drug holidays, and attempt to discontinue the med when the targeted behavior no
longer exists, unless *medically contraindicated*. I had the opportunity to ask the New York State Health Department what was meant
by *medically contraindicated*. If one has made two attempts to
lower the dosage unsuccessfully, than one could deem it *medically
contraindicated* to make any further attempts. If this is the case, it
should be documented in the medical record.

An example of proper documentation is as follows:

> The patient is displaying psychotic features of dementia.
> He is delusional and believes his deceased mother needs
> him at home. He tries to bolt the institution and assaults
> staff when redirected. Social service consult and counsel-
> ing has been ineffective. Discussed risks, alternatives, and
> benefits with family, including no treatment at all. Family
> concurs with an attempt to start Seroquel 25mg, bid to
> target these behaviors, and taper accordingly.

Failure to act in this manner may unnecessarily increase a physician's liability.

Liability has also increased in the arena of patient restraints. In the 1970s, lawsuits were filed due to injuries because restraints *were not* used. In the 1990s, lawsuits were filed due to injuries because restraints *were* used. It may be difficult for the family to comprehend why a confused loved one, without restraints, fell out of bed and fractured a hip. The explanation that the risk of serious injury and/or death by strangulation is even greater with restraints, and that federal guidelines discourage restraints, may not be acceptable to them. One suggestion to possibly limit liability is to notify family that you are a *restraint free facility* at the time of admission and have them sign off on the policy.

Another common cause of nursing home liability is when a resident falls. We are all aware of the multiple factors contributing to falls, some of which are: sundowning symptoms, psychotropic use, sedating meds, anti-hypertensive, gait disorders, impaired vision, slippery floors, staffing patterns, etc. Studies in nursing homes reveal that approximately one fall per patient bed per year is common.

As chairman of the QA committee, I conducted a comprehensive investigation into our falls. I examined all of the potential causes previously listed. Although there was a higher incidence of falls during evenings and weekends when staffing was low, my overall conclusion was that *residents in nursing homes fall.*

Even though falls are ubiquitous, we all need to make further attempts to reduce serious injuries. We have provided anti-slip stockings to all of our residents. In some facilities in England, mattresses are kept on the floor to prevent fractured hips. Perhaps someone will devise a nursing home bed that can be electronically lowered near the floor at bedtime.

If your facility has a problem with falls, I would recommend a comprehensive study on the subject. When the New York State

Health Department asked what was being done to rectify the situation, I referred to the 75-page study conducted on the subject. Would such a study reduce liability? It certainly can't hurt.

In the past, nursing home practice was an area of relatively low liability since patients had no significant loss of income and most patients had a limited life expectancy. However, recent court rulings and plaintiff awards have now changed that. As a result, many physicians have either curtailed or suspended care of the elderly in our nursing homes.

PEARL AND PITFALL: Plaintiff awards have increased in nursing home cases due to alleged inadequate pain control, use of psychotropics, restraint usage and falls; therefore physicians need to monitor these issues closely.

25

Don't Overstate Your Qualifications

A WOMAN BROUGHT HER YOUNG daughter to the ER with a facial laceration. The ER doctor gave the patient the option of having him repair the wound or requesting a plastic surgeon. The mom selected the latter. The ER doctor referred to the schedule to see who was covering plastics, and called the physician. The laceration was repaired, and the patient was referred back to her primary for follow up. At the follow-up visit, the mom expressed no evidence of dissatisfaction until her doctor said, "Not a bad job for a dermatologist." The mom was appalled, stating "I specifically requested a plastic surgeon." Apparently in this relatively small hospital, the only plastic surgeon shared emergency on-call with the sole dermatologist. The family filed a malpractice suit, which I was told was settled out of court.

Let us assume that you are an Internist and completed one year of a two-year cardiology fellowship. Many of your patients refer to you as their cardiologist. Take precautions that you do not advertise yourself as a cardiologist or endorse that misconception. A preferable approach would be to refer to yourself as an internist with special interest in cardiac disorders. If you find yourself in court, exaggerating your credentials may adversely affect the outcome.

PEARL AND PITFALL: Marketing yourself with credentials beyond your training can be an invitation to disaster.

26

Patient Confidentiality vs. the Public's Right to Know

IN A FAMOUS LANDMARK CASE, a mentally distressed patient, who was under the care of a psychiatrist, expressed recurrent thoughts of murdering his estranged girlfriend. The physician did not share these thoughts with the woman or the authorities. The patient acted upon his obsession and murdered the woman.

The family sued the psychiatrist for malpractice. The physician claimed doctor-patient confidentiality as his defense. The court didn't buy it, ruling that the "*public's right to know*" outweighed the issue of confidentiality. The physician had an obligation to notify the woman and the authorities that the patient was planning a crime. Incidentally, the same ruling has been applied to the clergy and the legal profession as well. Once again, physicians are faced with a dilemma: the need to weigh issues of confidentiality versus public interest. If the physician had notified the authorities, and the patient took no action on those threats, could the physician have possibly found himself in the position of defending a suit for breaching patient confidentiality?

PEARL AND PITFALL: When confronted with the choice of confidentiality or the *public's right to know*, seek legal advice from your insurance carrier.

27

Retain Your Medical Records

MANY PHYSICIANS ARE UNAWARE of the need to retain copies of their records after retiring or discontinuing their practice. A variety of individuals and institutions may request to review or subpoena those records, amongst which are malpractice attorneys, your insurance carrier, federal narcotics investigators, Medicare, other financial audits, or the patients themselves. Certain records such as HIV testing and employee needle sticks need to be retained for up to 30 years.

I know of several retired physicians who simply requested patients "to come in and pick up their charts," without retaining any record of the chart for their own future benefit. The potential liability of this may be devastating. How could one defend oneself against a malpractice suit or a financial audit without such records?

If you do discontinue your practice, my recommendation would be for the physician to have a staff member available for 30 days after closing the office solely for the purpose of copying charts upon request. A physician may charge up to 75 cents per page to copy records in New York State (may vary in other states), which I would recommend waiving in cases of financial hardship. Ads should be placed in local newspapers, and/or notices sent to your patients notifying them of your policy. After that period, I would make arrangements with an area institution or another physician to act as custodian of the records. Furthermore, I would request that the keeper of the records sign an agreement that they bear responsibility for retaining the records and making copies available to the patient or by subpoena.

PEARL AND PITFALL: Never surrender your records without retaining a copy or appointing a custodian of the records.

28

When the Press Calls

IF AND WHEN THE PRESS CALLS you for a statement, give careful consideration to your response. Newspapers like provocative and flamboyant headlines and often put their own slant on stories. A colleague of mine became outraged when he made a statement to the press and then claimed he was grossly misquoted.

I personally learned to beware of the press from my own unfortunate experience when a student at City College of New York. The professor didn't like the dusty basement room assigned for our English class and so she decided to hold the class of ten students in the cafeteria. A reporter from the school paper heard about it from one of our classmates and thought it would make a nice feature story. The article was written in a very critical manner toward the teacher. She, in turn, stated that it would be nice if all of us wrote to the Editor in her defense stating how much we were learning in this relaxed atmosphere. It wasn't until the day of class while hanging onto a subway strap that I realized I had forgotten to write the letter and so I hastily scribbled something down and sent it in.

My letter was published as written, including the "(*sic*)"s showing the spelling and grammatical errors. The professor's embarrassment was now even greater, to say nothing about my own misfortune. (It was the only C I ever received at CCNY.) Where was Spell Check when I needed it?

After hearing about other claims of being misquoted, I adopted the following policy. When my secretary informs me that the press is requesting a statement, she first tells them that I am unavailable at that time. However, if they ask their question, I will get back to them. After I prepare the statement, I have my secretary read it back to the press and then send them the statement. That way, I cannot be misquoted, and have a copy of my verbatim statement.

PEARL AND PITFALL: When the press calls, take precautions not to be misquoted.

29

The Mind of the Plaintiff

THERE ARE A VARIETY OF REASONS why your patient may turn into the plaintiff. Some of these can be attributed to the patient's state of mind, and were alluded to in Chapter 6, "Bedside Manner vs. Do You Care?"

It would be judicious not to make the patient feel guilty for his or her condition. Don't say, "If you took better care of yourself, this wouldn't have happened." Many lawsuits result due to a feeling of guilt from either the patient or family. Guilt can have an overwhelming effect on one's psyche. It can readily lead to depression, insomnia, rumination, anxiety, and then a need to act out. Those suffering from guilt may feel an intense need to transfer these negative feelings from themselves to others.

Sometimes, such feelings are due to actions or inactions taken during the loved one's illness, whereas, other times, guilt is attributable to a sense of shame for wanting to experience pleasure after a loved one has departed. Many patients suffer from depression, which goes beyond the acute brief transient situational reaction.

Although every case differs, I have found one approach to assist many such patients manage these feelings. I would say, "You and your spouse have had a wonderful life together. No one can take those memories away. However, I suspect that if your spouse had one final wish, it would be that you make the most of the remainder of your life. Go out, make friends, do things and have fun. Isn't that what your spouse would want?"

I have said this to my patients because I believe it is the truth. It would be what I would want for my wife, as well. Furthermore, I have detected a significant relief from sensations of guilt, and an improved mental outlook after such advice. Also, a patient not dwelling in guilt has fewer tendencies to seek the services of an attorney to alleviate these feelings.

Another reason that may send your patient to an attorney is a failure of a physician to acknowledge an error. If you have made an error that has caused injury or harm to your patient, the best course of action, after consulting with your attorney, may be a concise explanation of the error, followed by an apology. For many patients, that is all they want to hear.

PEARL AND PITFALL: A sense of guilt may contribute to your patient becoming a plaintiff.

30

Tort Reform: Hopefully Sooner than Later

THE CURRENT SYSTEM IS FAULTY and in need of considerable revision, not only for the sake of physicians but for their patients as well. Awards for pain and suffering need to have realistic caps. Presenting complex medical decisions whereby expert witnesses drastically state opposing conclusions and then rely on lay juries to find the truth is an antiquated approach for managing complex problems.

Someday, hopefully, a more equitable and just system will be implemented. One such approach would adopt a *No Fault* system similar to the automotive industry. Allegations of malpractice would be presented to a Board consisting of physicians, state health department officials, and other licensing agencies. Unfortunately, the recent health care law has failed to address any of these malpractice issues.

The facts of the case and testimony from unbiased specialty physicians would be reviewed, along with considering the physician's training, experience, and patterns of care. Does the physician have a pattern of providing substandard care, or are the findings an isolated incident? Physicians found to have a pattern of poor care or otherwise deemed incompetent should be weeded out of the system with license suspension or revocation.

PEARL AND PITFALL: If we are unable to revise the current system many excellent physicians will leave the profession and the cost of medical care in this country will continue to rise at an even higher unacceptable rate. As physicians, we have the responsibility to speak out against an unworkable and unjust system. We need to educate our patients and the public, encourage them to write their Congressmen, and continue to pressure our legislatures to make changes in tort reform. Furthermore, changing the status quo would significantly curtail the practice of defensive medicine, resulting in enormous savings to both physicians and their patients by avoiding unnecessary malpractice suits.

CONCLUSION: We have entered into the most noble of all professions. Our goal has been to provide the best health and welfare for our patients. It is regrettable that our thoughts and actions are diverted by the need to practice defensive medicine to avoid malpractice suits. Hopefully, we can someday collectively help to reform the system so that we can spend all of our energies where they are best suited: the practice of medicine.

31

The Way It Should Be

Lori Ann Hertz

My daughter Heather died from AIDS in 1993. She lived until she was 12 years of age. This is the sad and inspiring story of the events that occurred starting with what caused the illness and details about Heather's care until her death.

Heather was born in 1981, a premature baby weighing only 2 lbs. 10 oz. She was perfect except for underdeveloped lungs which are considered normal for that birth weight. She was also anemic, and required blood transfusions. Heather was in the hospital for three months due to her low birth weight. After fully recovering from her premature lungs and anemia I was allowed to bring her home (at 5 lbs.) and begin life with my daughter as a perfectly healthy little baby girl. Before Heather reached the age of 12 months she had already had several colds, coughs and pneumonia. Initially, it was suspected that her premature birth caused the illnesses as HIV was not considered since she was not in a high risk group. During the mid 1980s I began to read about this virus called HIV which could be contracted from blood transfusions. Heather received blood in 1981 and the tests for this disease were not available until 1983.

This string of health problems continued until Heather was nine, when she developed oral thrush which I later learned occurs in people with suppressed immune function. At this point in time I decided to get another opinion. This new pediatric group tested her for HIV. The results came back positive! As long as I live, I will never forget the phone call I received from the new pediatrician (Dr. Michael) telling me to come in for the results. What followed changed my life and the lives of my entire family forever. My husband passed away when Heather was one and my son was five and the burden of caring for my family fell solely upon me.

Dr. Michael gently and compassionately told me the results, and asked that I find a pediatric infectious disease specialist for my daughter. Heather's HIV status had already progressed to the point of mid-stage AIDS. I interviewed three infectious disease doctors. Two of the waiting rooms felt like being in a third world country, with children moaning in pain and so sick they had to lie on the floor.

At the third hospital I went to I was introduced to a Dr. Robert. I was brought into a private room and Dr. Robert placed his hand on mine and said, "I will help you and Heather, and be with you every step of the way." I actually felt a ray of hope despite the severity of the diagnosis. And to say that Dr. Robert kept his word does not begin to describe the depth and breadth of his devotion, dedication, loyalty and compassion throughout Heather's battle with AIDS.

For the next three and one-half years I did nothing but take care of Heather, work at my business as a designer, and take care of my older son who at that point was placed in a very good preparatory boarding school. I will not go into detail about all the invasive procedures Heather required or list all the scores of medications she daily ingested or describe the frequent hospitalizations.

I will however, describe the care and support my daughter received from all the doctors and nurses that we dealt with for the remaining years of her life. They were nothing short of extraordinary. Dr. Robert (the infectious diseases doctor) came to my home so Heather wouldn't miss school when she needed blood drawn, which occurred three times per week. Her new pediatrician (Dr. Michael) would meet us in the hospital just to talk and see how we were doing.

My daughter received the best unwavering care any patient could hope for and any doctor could provide. They researched all available new medications and left no stone unturned to insure she had the best quality of life for her remaining years. Whenever Heather needed treatment for her lungs Dr. Robert would sit with Heather and hold her hand or rub her arms as to distract her. He was an angel. The doctors and nurses would bring over flowers, send get-well cards, buy small toys and were always available for my numerous daily phone calls and concerns. They had the patience of saints.

I called Dr. Robert every day with another treatment I read about. His response was always, "fax it to me and I will read it and we can discuss the pros and cons of this particular trial." I don't know how he found the time to be as accommodating as he was, for Heather was not his only patient, but we were made to feel like she was.

I only wish that more doctors would understand the importance of non-medical care. Patients want to feel heard. Doctors will often *hear* a patient's concerns and complaints but will not *listen* to other extenuating factors. I was completely psychologically devastated. My raw emotions were exposed as never before. These physicians took me under their wings and helped me cope. I leaned on them both literally and figuratively on a daily basis. I questioned everything and was encouraged to get second opinions.

Heather was a brave and remarkable little girl. She would say to me, "Mommy, it is so unfair for you to have a sick child like me." I never would have had the strength to endure the loss of a child without the love and support of the doctors and nurses that I relied on during the most horrific years of my life. And I certainly wouldn't have traded Heather for anything in the world.

When I asked Heather's doctors why they all became so involved, allowing their own emotions to be touched, they replied, "Heather is the little girl that everyone wants to have as their own child." She never complained. She was always appreciative. She would ask her doctors how they were doing because she genuinely cared about them and she felt their reciprocity. She connected with them as loving and caring human beings. It is understood that doctors cannot get this involved with all their patients as it would become too emotionally taxing; however, they did in this case.

When Heather succumbed to her disease at age twelve the doctors were there to support me once again. They attended the funeral, they cried, they wrote poems, they sent flowers, paid their respects, and grieved with me.

Years after Heather passed away I was asked to speak to the pediatric infectious disease residents at New York University Hospital on the topic of doctor–patient relationships. The questions posed to me were varied and numerous. I told the story just as I told it here. One doctor stood up and admitted that he was in the wrong field of medicine and could not deal with the death of a child. Questions and concerns such as these should be asked not only in medical schools but throughout a doctor's life.

I hope that my experience will touch physicians and increase their awareness to show compassion, support and patience with those in need. For Heather and myself, it was a positive life-altering experience.

DR. JOSHPE'S POSTSCRIPT: I hope that everyone who reads Lori and Heather's story will be touched by it and will learn from it as well. I certainly have. Yes, mistakes will be made in medicine, since we physicians are human beings. We do not have all of the answers. Every case does not have a happy ending. We cannot predict the effect of every drug or procedure that we administer. And yet, how can anyone reading this story not appreciate the caring and the compassion given to Heather by her care givers?

Even if one hypothetically envisioned an error in the care of such a patient, would anyone ever consider instituting a charge of malpractice? *I doubt it very much.*

PEARL AND PITFALL: As physicians, we need to constantly bear in mind the needs, the fears, and the sense of isolation experienced by our patients, and be willing to share those feelings with them. Their pain needs to be our pain as well. If we can learn to think and act in this manner, our thoughts and fears of malpractice will begin to dissipate.

32

True or False Quiz

Place a T for true or F for false, next to the corresponding numbered statement.

1. ___ Patients seen in the ER should be told to follow up with their primary doctor at their convenience.

2. ___ Physicians tend to provide their best care to their loved ones.

3. ___ If one falls behind schedule and patients are waiting excessively, either the physician or a staff member should notify those in the waiting room and apologize.

4. ___ In Malcolm Gladwell's book, *Blink*, he reveals a direct relationship between a physician's training and malpractice events.

5. ___ One can never predict with confidence which patient may subsequently become a plaintiff.

6. ____ The QA committee is the proper venue for discussing concerns of quality care.

7. ____ When one discovers a quality of care issue in the surgical tissue committee, that finding should never leave that committee.

8. ____ When a physician applies for privileges to several hospitals simultaneously, it is not necessary for each facility to perform their own independent credentials check.

9. ____ When using a form to check screening guidelines the best method is to attach the form to the patient's chart, even if you don't refer to it.

10. ____ When using abbreviations include your abbreviation list in your policies and procedures.

11. ____ When working up a patient, only mention one specific diagnosis, rather than listing other possible disease entities.

12. ____ A physician has a responsibility to enter into a *doctor-patient relationship* when it is requested by a patient.

13. ____ When a patient requests their records all information in the chart should be sent.

14. ____ Before sending out patient records they should be reviewed carefully, and all errors should be crossed out.

15. ____ Employing a mid-level may put you at an increased risk of liability for their errors.

16. ___ In medicine you can easily predict which cases will turn out to be uncomplicated.

17. ___ When caring for a flirtatious patient, always have a staff member in the exam room during the examination.

18. ___ If you believe the patient is a hypochondriac, you should mention that in the medical record.

19. ___ It is the responsibility of the primary care physician to follow up on all tests ordered by a consultant or a referral physician, and notify the patient of the results.

20. ___ If you disagree with decisions made by the patient's previous physician, you should state this in the medical record.

21. ___ Physicians would do best to concentrate on what they do well, and seek consultation or referral in areas out of the area of expertise.

22. ___ When a physician is out of the office, it is not necessary to document phone calls from patients.

23. ___ Residents in nursing homes should never be given narcotics for pain, since that may contribute to falls.

24. ___ Restraints should routinely be ordered for nursing home residents who are at high risk for falls.

25. ___ The most serious injuries in nursing homes occur in residents with restraints as opposed to those without restraints.

26. ____ With proper medical and nursing care, the vast number of falls in nursing homes can be eliminated.

27. ____ Use of psychotropic medications contributes to falls in nursing home residents.

28. ____ If a psychiatrist believes a patient is about to commit murder, the responsibility to notify authorities exceeds the responsibility of *doctor-patient confidentiality*.

29. ____ A physician has the responsibility to immediately notify the patient of any error made, regardless of its consequences.

30. ____ A physician should consult with their insurance carrier before discussing potential malpractice with the patient's attorney.

31. ____ A physician who retires has the responsibility to assure that a copy of the patient's record is retained.

32. ____ If a patient becomes angry with his or her physician because they contracted lung cancer, the physician should mention that his or her decision to smoke contributed to the disease.

33. ____ If a patient refuses to schedule a colonoscopy as recommended, it is best to document that in the medical record, and have the patient initial the entry.

34. ___ If you make an error in the medical record, it is acceptable to erase the error when done on the same day as the patient's visit.

35. ___ A physician who terminates a doctor-patient relationship must give the patient seven days notice to find a new doctor.

36. ___ Regardless of whether you request a consult or a referral from another physician, your responsibilities to the patient are the same.

37. ___ When your medical records are subpoenaed, you are required to forward the entire record, including notes from the patient's previous physicians.

38. ___ A physician bears no responsibility for arranging a follow-up visit for a patient treated in the ER.

39. ___ Once a physician writes a prescription for a patient, a *doctor-patient relationship* has been established.

40. ___ A physician may utilize one abbreviation for two separate items, provided both are listed in the official abbreviation list.

33
Answers to Quiz

1.	F	2.	F	3.	T	4.	F	5.	T	6.	T	7.	F	8.	F
9.	F	10.	T	11.	F	12.	F	13.	F	14.	F	15.	T	16.	F
17.	T	18.	F	19.	F	20.	F	21.	T	22.	F	23.	F	24.	F
25.	T	26.	F	27.	T	28.	T	29.	F	30.	T	31.	T	32.	F
33.	T	34.	F	35.	F	36.	F	37.	F	38.	F	39.	T	40.	F

www.ingramcontent.com/pod-product-compliance
Lightning Source LLC
Chambersburg PA
CBHW022116170526
45157CB00004B/1667